MONEY MATTERS

What's It Worth?

Financial Literacy

Torrey Maloof

Consultants

Michele Ogden, Ed.D
Principal, Irvine Unified School District

Jennifer Robertson, M.A.Ed.
Teacher, Huntington Beach City School District

Publishing Credits

Rachelle Cracchiolo, M.S.Ed., *Publisher*
Conni Medina, M.A.Ed., *Managing Editor*
Dona Herweck Rice, *Series Developer*
Emily R. Smith, M.A.Ed., *Series Developer*
Diana Kenney, M.A.Ed., NBCT, *Content Director*
Kevin Panter, *Graphic Designer*
Stacy Monsman, M.A., *Editor*

Image Credits: p. 11 Portra Images/Getty Images; pp. 20–21 Education Images/UIG via Getty Images; p. 23 Catchlight Visual Services/Alamy Stock Photo; pp. 24-25 NurPhoto.com/Alamy Stock Photo; all other images from iStock and/or Shutterstock.

Library of Congress Cataloging-in-Publication Data
Names: Maloof, Torrey.
Title: Money matters : what's it worth? / Torrey Maloof.
Description: Huntington Beach, CA : Teacher Created Materials, [2017] | Audience: K to grade 3. | Includes index. | Description based on print version record and CIP data provided by publisher; resource not viewed.
Identifiers: LCCN 2017007842 (print) | LCCN 2016053558 (ebook) | ISBN 9781480758704 (eBook) | ISBN 9781480758063 (pbk.)
Subjects: LCSH: Finance, Personal--Juvenile literature. | Money--Juvenile literature. | Addition--Juvenile literature.
Classification: LCC HG179 (print) | LCC HG179 .M25724 2017 1995 (ebook) | DDC 332.024--dc23
LC record available at https://lccn.loc.gov/2017007842

Teacher Created Materials
5301 Oceanus Drive
Huntington Beach, CA 92649-1030
http://www.tcmpub.com

ISBN 978-1-4807-5806-3

Printed by 51250
PO48266 / Printed in USA

Table of Contents

Money Matters

Imagine you are at your favorite store. You have a crisp, clean $10 bill in your hand. You also have a quarter, a dime, a nickel, and a penny. As you look down at Mr. Hamilton's face on the $10 bill, you start asking yourself questions. What can I **afford** to buy? Should I buy something fun that I really want? Or, should I buy something **practical** that I need? There are many things to think about when it comes to money.

Money is a tool. It is important to use that tool properly. To do so, you must understand money's **value**. You need to know what money means to you. Once you know all the ins and outs of money, you will be able to use it wisely and make smart choices. That way, you can get the most bang for your buck!

LET'S EXPLORE MATH

These are the featured products at a toy store:

1,000 piece puzzle	$3
comic book	$5
engineering kit	$20
pack of bubblegum	$1
reusable water bottle	$7
solar-powered dancing monkey	$2
super hero T-shirt	$10

1. If you have $10 to spend, which items can you afford to buy? Are there any items you cannot afford to buy?
2. How many ways can you buy 3 different items without spending more than $10?
3. Can you buy 3 items and spend exactly $10? Prove your reasoning.

Value Choices

Does your family use paper towels? Maybe there is a roll in your kitchen. Did you know there are different **brands** of paper towels? Some are more **expensive** than others. If a paper towel is made of thick paper it may **cost** more. Thin paper towels tend to cost less. Which should you buy? Which brand is the better value? The more costly paper towels may work better. So, the roll may last longer. Or, you may want to spend less money. But, those paper towels may not work as well.

People have to make choices like this every day. Using money wisely can be a challenge. But, the more you know about the value of money, the more it will make sense. Let's take a closer look at some real-life money matters.

LET'S EXPLORE MATH

You conducted an experiment to see which brand of paper towels is the better value for your family. Use the data to decide which brand your family should buy. Why do you think so?

Brand	Price	Quantity	Time
Tough Towels	$3	1 roll	6 days
Simple Sheets	$1	1 roll	4 days

Family Finances

Meet Carl. He's ten years old and loves nothing more than playing basketball. Shooting hoops is his life. He hopes to be a professional basketball player one day.

Carl's mom works hard at her job. She works long hours. She does not make much money, but she makes enough to **provide** for the two of them.

Carl plays on a basketball team with students from his school. They all have the latest and greatest basketball shoes—the Air Zone Max! The shoes are stylish, sturdy, and just plain cool. Carl wants a pair badly, but he knows they are very expensive. He knows he will never be able to afford them with his allowance. So, he decides to ask his mom if she will buy the shoes for him.

One night after dinner, Carl tells his mom about the basketball shoes. She begins the discussion by asking him a series of questions. *Why do you need them? Are they made well? How much do they cost?*

Carl explains that he wants the shoes simply because everyone else on his team has them. He knows they won't make him play better, but he thinks they will make him happy and give him more confidence on the court. He tells her they are made very well. They are durable and will last a long time. They won't rip or tear easily. Then, he takes a deep breath and tells her how much they cost—$200!

Carl's mom knows how her son feels. So, she goes over the family **finances** with him. She takes out a pad of paper. She writes how much she makes and how many hours she works a week. Carl and his mom use math to find out how many hours she would have to work to pay for the shoes.

Then, she explains that money gets taken out of her paychecks for **taxes**. After that, she has to pay for their home, food, and other **expenses**. Carl learns it will take a long time and a lot of hard work to get those shoes. Carl really wants the Air Zone Max shoes, but he now realizes that he values how hard his mom works more than the shoes.

earnings per hour: $20

$20 x 10 hours = $200

hours worked to afford shoes: 10

other expenses:

- taxes
- bills
- rent
- food
- utilities

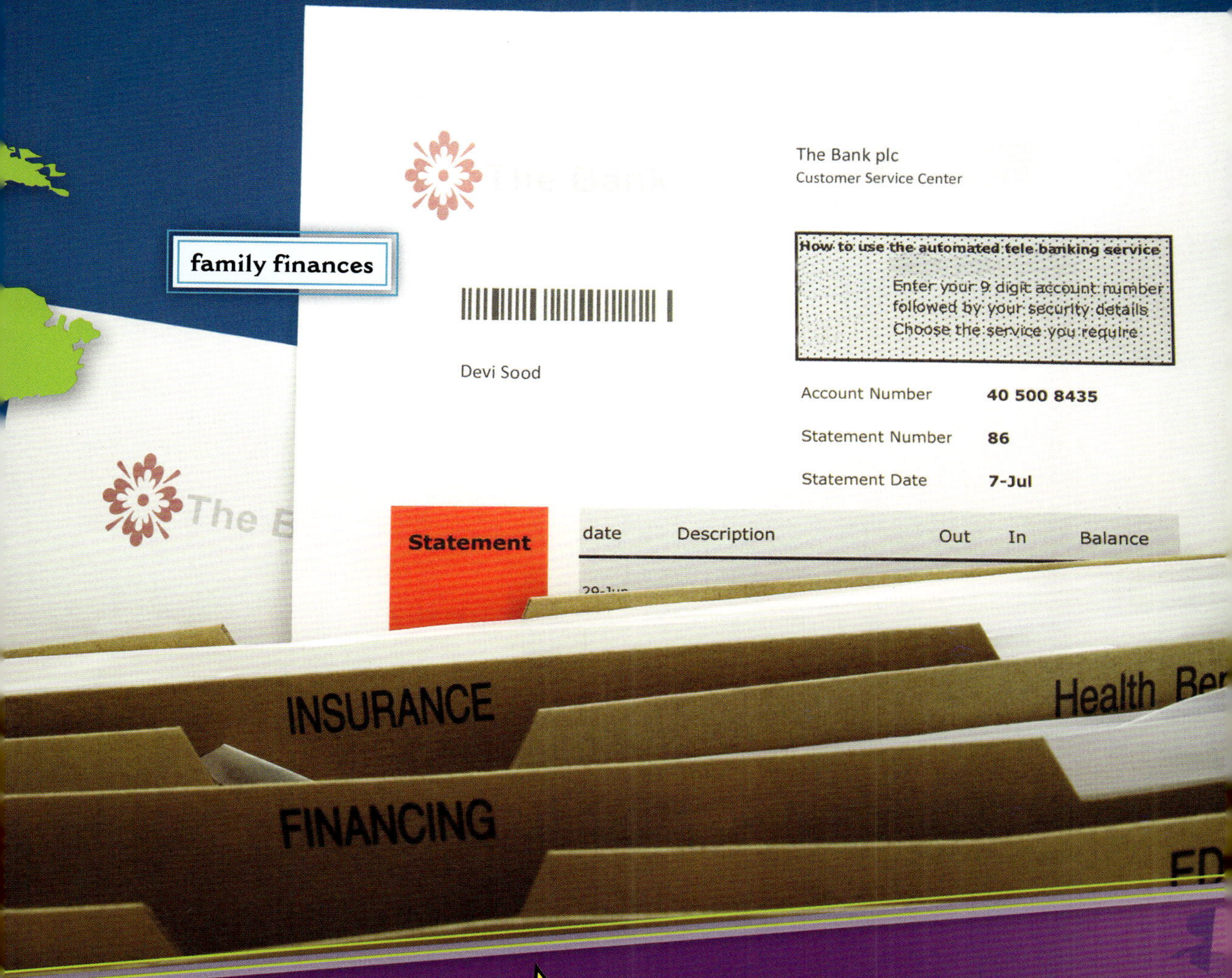

family finances

LET'S EXPLORE MATH

There's a new space alien movie you want to see. Some people have said it's great. Others have said it is horrible. It will cost you $10 to see the movie. You have to do 5 hours of chores to earn $10. Do you think seeing the movie is a good value for your money? Would you change your mind if you only had to work one hour to earn $10? Explain your thinking.

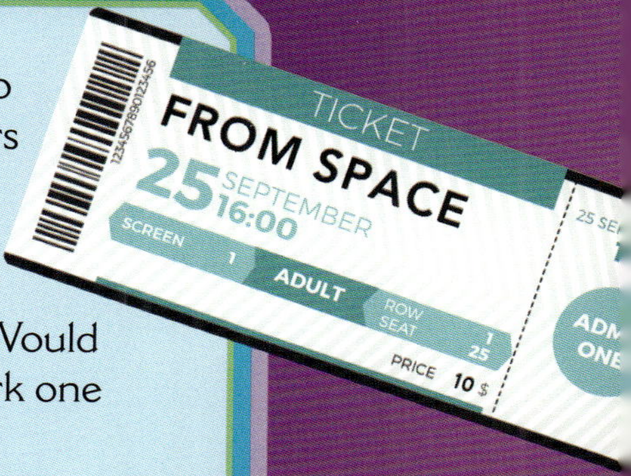

Buying a Bike

Amal's best friend Gracie is moving. Her new home is all the way across town. Amal won't be able to walk to Gracie's house anymore. Gracie is also starting a new school. Amal can't imagine not seeing her best friend each day. They have been best friends since they were three years old.

Amal tries to think of ways she can still see Gracie. Her father says she's not old enough to ride the city bus alone. He also tells her that he won't drive her to Gracie's house every day. She keeps thinking. She decides she will buy a bike.

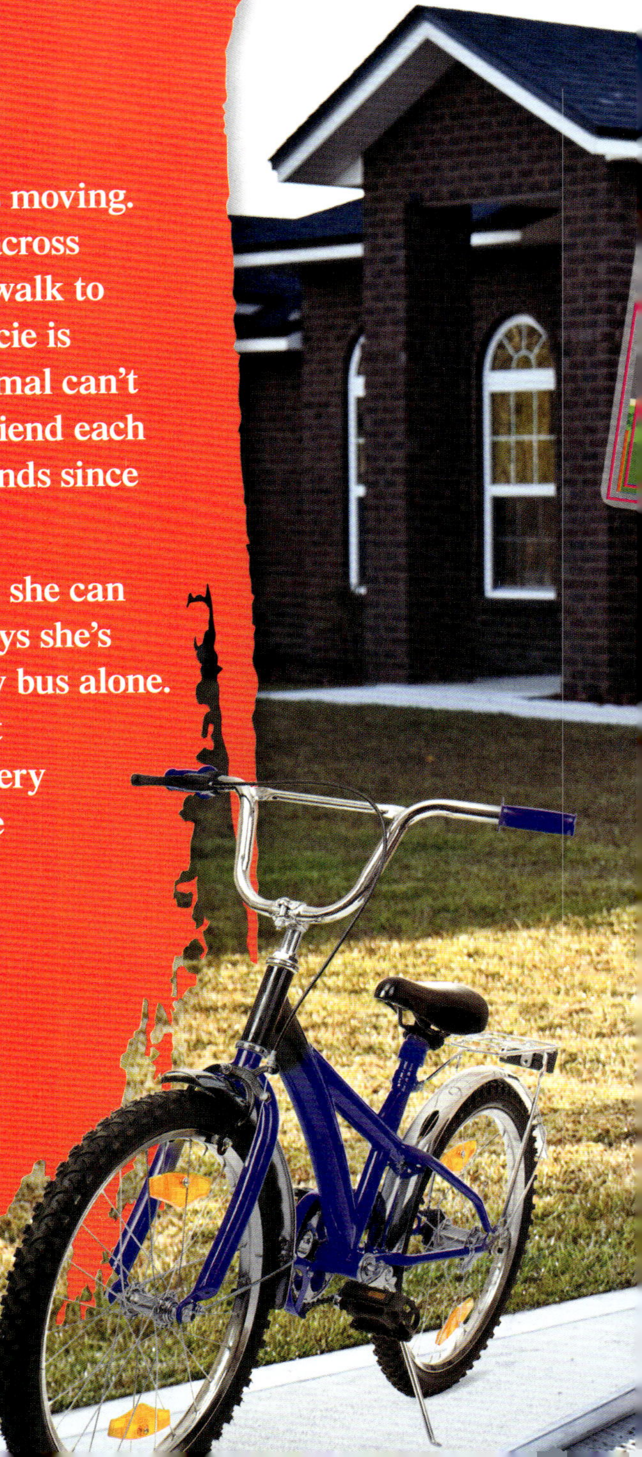

Gracie's house
Amal's house

Amal's dad thinks buying a bike is a great idea. But, he tells her that she will have to pay for it herself. She will need to earn the money. She can do extra chores around the house. He thinks this will be a great **opportunity** for her. She will learn about earning and saving money. And, she will understand the value of money.

Amal and her dad make a plan.

Amal's Chores

Chore	Payment	Time Required
mow lawn		
vacuum		
dusting		
take out trash		
cook dinner		
mop the floor		
wash the car		

Amal's chore chart

The two sit down together. They make a chore chart. A **monetary** value is written next to each chore. An **estimated** time is written, too. This way, Amal will have an idea of how much time it will take her to earn the money she needs to purchase the bike.

Amal looks at bikes online. She reads reviews to decide which bike will be the best fit for her. She compares prices on different sites to find the best deal. Finally, she chooses the Nova Sky Cruiser 2000.

Amal and her dad go to the store to get a closer look at the bike. She asks the salesperson questions. She rides the bike around the store to make sure she likes it.

The bike is expensive. It costs $125. Amal will have to work hard and save her money for quite some time. She will have to make sacrifices. This means not spending her money on other things, such as movie tickets and candy. But, she thinks it will be worth it because she will get to see her best friend. For her, it is a good value.

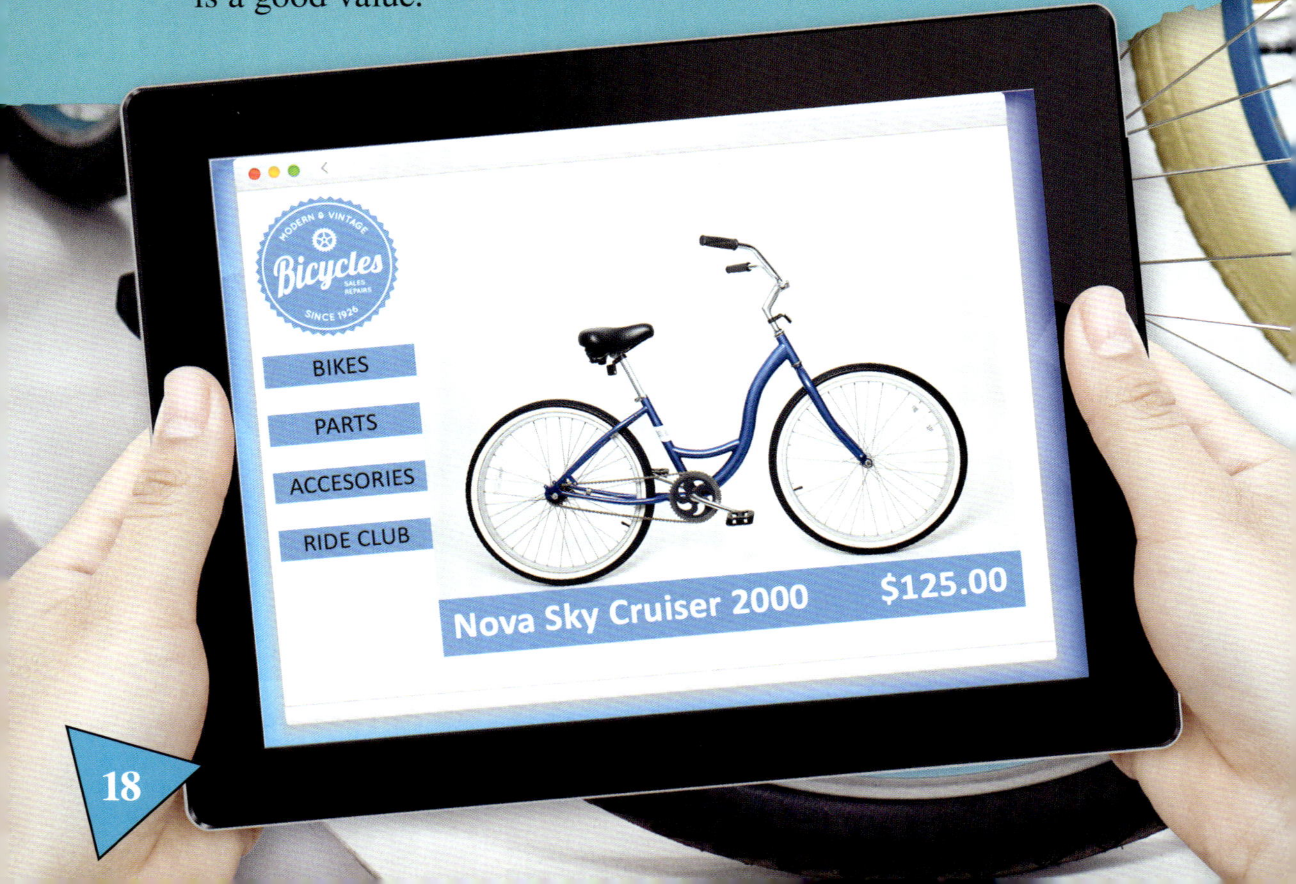

LET'S EXPLORE MATH

Amal made a chart of chores she could do to earn $125. Design a plan that will help her meet her goal. Remember, she can complete chores more than once.

Chore	Payment	Time Required
mow lawn	$15	2 hours
vacuum	$3	30 minutes
dusting	$2	15 minutes
take out trash	$3	10 minutes
cook dinner	$10	1 hour
mop the floor	$7	1 hour
wash the car	$12	2 hours

1. Which chores could she do to earn $125? How many hours will it take her to complete those chores?
2. How often could she do each of the chores? How long will it take her to earn $125?

Saving for the Shelter

Raj enjoys earning his own money. It makes him feel good about himself. When he was a child, he walked the neighborhood dogs. When he got older, he began to pet sit for his neighbors. Today, he's 16 years old and has a part-time job after school. He works at the Cozy Cat Rescue Center.

Raj loves his job. He respects his boss and likes playing with and taking care of the cats. His favorite part is when a loving family adopts a cat. The only part Raj does not like is that the cats are kept in small cages. He wants to change that.

Raj does some research. He learns about cage-free shelters. In these types of shelters, cats are not kept in cages. Instead, they are free to roam in home-like environments. There are big rooms with cat beds and toys. The cats are allowed to mix and mingle; they can play with each other and have fun.

Raj tells his boss about the cage-free environment. She loves the idea but says she does not have the money or time to make it happen. Raj volunteers to help. He says he can also **donate** his **wages**. His boss is thrilled with Raj's passion and generosity. She tells him to draw up a plan and a **budget** for her to review and approve.

Raj's boss feeds the cats.

Raj makes some phone calls. He learns how much the remodel will cost. He estimates it will be about $1,500. Raj works only 10 hours a week. He makes $10 an hour. It will take him almost four months to earn the money.

Raj would like to build the new playroom sooner rather than later. So, he decides to hold a **fundraiser**. People like to donate money. It makes them feel good. It adds a special value to their money. It is nice to help others who need it, including animals. Raj presents his ideas and budget to his boss. She loves it. She approves his plan!

Just two months later, the cats at the Cozy Cat Rescue Center are enjoying their new pad—all thanks to Raj and his savvy financial sense.

A volunteer plays with the cats in their new playroom.

LET'S EXPLORE MATH

Think about what you learned about Raj's finances from the text. Use that information to answer the questions below.

1. How much money does Raj make for one week's work? How do you know?
2. If Raj donates all his earnings for 7 weeks, how much will he donate? Show your thinking.
3. Raj needs $1,500. He donates 7 weeks worth of his earnings. How much does he need to make from the fundraiser? How do you know?

Thinking It Through

The best way to get the most value for your money is to make sense of it. Think about what it takes to earn that money. It is important to ask yourself questions. Will you have to work hard, or will the work be easy? Will it take you a long time to reach your goal, or will you reach it quickly? Did someone else have to work hard to give you that money? Should you save it, spend it, or donate it? There are many big decisions to make.

The next time you hold a $10 bill in your hand, think about it. Think about what it means to you and how you can use it wisely. How will you get the most value out of your money?

Problem Solving

Annie is planning her summer. She wants to play with friends. But, she also wants to work to earn some money. Annie wants to split her money equally between three things. She wants to put part of her earnings into a savings account. She wants to donate part of her money to her school. And, she wants to spend the rest of her money on fun activities with her friends!

Annie looks for summer jobs in her community. She makes a table of the jobs she has found. It shows how much they pay and how many hours she will work. Use the table to help you solve the problems.

1. How many hours will Annie work this summer? How do you know?
2. At which job will Annie earn the most money? How do you know?
3. How much money will Annie make in total? Explain your reasoning.
4. How much money will Annie save, spend, and donate? Explain the steps you took to answer this question.
5. Do you think Annie understands the value of money? Why or why not?

Jobs	Pay per Hour	Hours
walk dog	$5	4
mow lawn	$8	3
wash dishes	$2	8

Glossary

afford—to be able to pay for something

brands—kinds of products or goods made by specific companies

budget—a plan for using money over a period of time

cost—to have an amount of money as a price

donate—to give something such as time or money to help another person

estimated—to have guessed a value based on observation and information

expenses—money spent regularly to pay for things

expensive—costing a lot of money; a high price

finances—money available to a person, business, or government

fundraiser—an event held to collect money for a charity

monetary—relating to money

opportunity—a chance or situation to better oneself

practical—reasonable to use or do

provide—to supply what is needed for someone to live

taxes—an amount of money the government requires people pay based on their income

value—the worth of something

wages—the amount of money a worker is paid

Index

Answer Key

Let's Explore Math

page 5:

1. You can afford everything except the engineering kit.
2. 5 ways
3. water bottle, monkey, gum ($7 + $2 + $1 = $10); or, puzzle, comic book, monkey ($3 + $5 + $2 = $10)

page 7:

Example: My family should buy Simple Sheets because the cost per day is 25¢, or 1 quarter. Tough Towels is more because the cost per day is 50¢, or 2 quarters.

page 13:

Example: I wouldn't see the movie if it took 5 hours of chores because the movie is only 2 hours long. I'd see the movie if it only took 1 hour to earn the money.

page 19:

1. Chores listed will vary but value should total $125 or more. Hours will depend on chores listed.
2. Hours and time will vary based on chores chosen.

page 25:

1. $100; $10 x 10 hours = $100
2. $700; $100 x 7 weeks = $700
3. $800; $1,500 – $700 = $800

Problem Solving

1. 15 hours; 4 + 3 + 8 = 15
2. Mowing lawns because $8 x 3 hours = $24, while $5 x 4 hours = $20 and $2 x 8 hours = $16
3. $60; $20 + $24 + $16 = $60
4. Save $20, spend $20, and donate $20; Steps will vary.
5. Example: I think Annie understands the value of money because she worked hard for her money and made carefully planned choices for spending it.